# Website Marketing Machine

**Get Your License To Drive Your Very Own**

**Website Marketing Machine!**

*No Experience Required*

Albert L. Powell, Jr.

**ISBN:9798617458994**

**Visit Our Homepage:** http://www.websitemarketingmachine.com.

## DEDICATION

This book is dedicated to my brother Steve, who blazed the marketing trail practically all his life. With his charismatic style, he built relationships all over the world. Even though he departed this earth way too early, I was able to learn from him some secrets that continue to help me today.

This book is proof that applying the fundamentals will work for anyone who wants to take the time to learn and practice them. I cannot count the hours my brother and I spent working on marketing strategies that were creative and well executed.

Steve would be proud to know that readers of this book won't have to spend all the time it took him to master the principles contained in this book. Years of hard work, trial, and error have been condensed to make it easier for anyone to grasp.

Rest in peace my dear brother, and know that your hard work has not gone in vain. It will be passed on to others who want to get results faster. Everything takes time, but with "Website Marketing Machine" to guide them, their ride will be a lot smoother.

In the marketing world, things change quickly. It's hard to stay on top of all the new marketing tools and techniques without continually augmenting your learning.

However, when you take the time to study and learn, it becomes an investment that will pay by producing better products and services, and ultimately by increasing your bottom line.

# ACKNOWLEDGEMENTS

Thanks to my family, friends , and fellow super achievers who are in the game of perfecting their skills to the level of mastery. Your candid explanations of your daily challenges have pushed me to continue writing this book.

I am blessed to have such a positive network of people that encourage and inspire me to perform at my very best. At times, I may sound like a broken record talking about the same things that excite me, but your patient listening means the world to me.

I only wish that you do see how much your input helps me go from one level of growth to the next. No man is an island, and when you have great support around you, nothing seems impossible.

A special thanks goes to my son, *Albert L. Powell, III.*, for generously taking time from his busy schedule to discuss issues that really matter.

He is always ready to go deeply on any subject that we discuss. Not only are his insights always on point, but also contain an element that inspires me to become better.

And a very special acknowledgment goes to my accountability partner, *Rose Smitherman,* who combines business savvy and common sense to every conversation that we have.

Her unwavering support, through good times and bad, will always be in the forefront of my thoughts.

I am forever grateful for her presence in my life that always prods me to keep moving forward even in the midst of insurmountable obstacles.

## ABOUT THIS BOOK

If you are new to marketing, or haven't had time to keep abreast of the whirlwind changes taking place these days, this book is for you. Everything is moving at such a fast pace that it can feel as if you've lost your license to drive on this new online marketing superhighway.

Don't worry, because this book will have you back on the digital marketing road in no time.

Just like studying to get your driver's license, once you know the fundamentals of driving, you can go anywhere. Online marketing is no different. The tools and methods of driving the superhighway are always changing, but the fundamentals never change.

Your ability to make money will depend on how well you drive your website marketing machine. Whether you drive fast or slow, to stay ahead today, you must keep the online marketing engine running.

Don't worry, because ***"Website Marketing Machine"*** is your all-in-one guide to get you up to speed. Not only are all the fundamentals covered, this book will get you versed in the new techniques needed to carry out a carefully targeted marketing strategy.

If you are a beginner trying to launch your very first product, or a seasoned veteran who's looking for a better online marketing approach, this book is for you.

As the manager of an entire marketing team, you will learn that the responsibility for marketing your business is no longer confined to the marketing department. Today, everyone in your organization should be involved in building the marketing message in everything they do.

The "Website Marketing Machine" is the vehicle that will drive your whole organization where you want to go. Once the marketing engine starts, you want it to run your marketing machine at high speeds, driving your organization to more and more profits. This book will jump-start your online marketing engine.

Online marketing can be intimidating at first, because there are so many components requiring various skills-sets. It can be confusing. Some aspects require highly technical skills, and others require lots of experience. But, this book will walk you, step-by-step, through the essential components that you need to get started.

Every good building is built upon a solid foundation, and that's exactly what this book will do for you. Keep building your knowledge chapter after chapter. Your "Website Marketing Machine" is ready to drive you anywhere you want to go.

All you need to do is turn the key.

## HOW TO USE THIS BOOK

As you go through this book, you will want to put together a strategy to glean the most information that you can. Reading it is one thing, but putting these concepts to practical use is what will make the biggest difference in your marketing.

The following are some quick tips on how you can approach your learning. The suggestions are as follows:

### As a Learning Guide

- Learn how to clearly define your audience

- Learn what it takes to put together a strategy to get started

- Learn how to set marketing goals and track them for results

- Learn to use email marketing, social media, and search marketing

- Learn how to dominate the channels that you're using

- Learn the importance of taking action and staying on course

- Learn to get additional information from the Website Marketing Machine blog

## As a Review Tool

Some of the concepts in this book you may already know. You may have even tried some channels and achieved some success.

If you are familiar with them, use this book as your review guide. The more you revisit what you already know, the stronger the learning becomes.

## As a Reference Guide

Even after you finish reading this book, keep it handy to use as your ready reference guide. There is a lot to learn and you will want to revisit this information often.

If you are working on a marketing campaign and you want to get a quick answer, feel free to go back to the book for a refresher. The more you expose yourself to the knowledge the better your retention.

Most of all, visit WebsiteMarketingMachine.com for even more support.

Our blog is loaded with timely articles that will keep you up to date.

Visit WebsiteMarketingMachine.com/blog.

# Table of Contents

## INTRODUCTION

The Internet has leveled the online marketing playing field. No matter what your size, you can market just like the major players in any industry. All it takes is some knowledge of digital marketing, creativity, and hard work.

Internet marketing is a cost effective way to launch and run successful marketing campaigns that get results. You can target more effectively to reach your valued audience. It makes it easy to measure your efforts, so you can continually get the most value for your investment.

This book will show you exactly what to do to make your website a resource that will educate your customers, giving them all the information they need to make an informed purchase.

Today, it's not only about getting customers to buy, it's about building long term relationships. As you provide the customer what they are looking for, you gain their trust. People like to do business with people they trust.

Throughout this book you will learn some absolute fundamentals of online marketing. You will learn how to generate visitors to your website, and turn those visitors into paying customers.

Although, the goal of the book is to teach you the techniques involved in online marketing, I want you to fully understand how to effectively use each one to maximize your marketing efforts.

Listed here are some of the techniques you'll learn:

- How to attract the exact customers you want by designing a professional website.

- How to begin a conversation with your customers through personalized email marketing.

- Why affiliate marketing with trusted partners is so important.

- How to choose the right online partners that complement what you do.

- How to use content marketing to attract visitors that will visit over and over again.

- How to brand yourself as an expert/influencer in your specific industry.

- How you can minimize your marketing budget while creating a dynamic reach through organic traffic.

Consider this book the start of your online marketing education that you will want to continue for the rest of your career. Learning something new everyday is a quick way to master these marketing techniques.

Once you have the fundamentals mastered, use them in any combination that works best. It's always advisable to do what works. So, make it a point to always test your efforts, and only repeat what is working.

Lastly, know that you can become a master at marketing, if you determine to never stop. Even when it doesn't look like you're making progress, determine to never stop. You will get the results you're after.

# Chapter One: The Benefits of Marketing Online

The world of online marketing is changing by the minute. As the Internet becomes more robust, and feature rich, so does the techniques involved in online marketing. With so many aspects to learn, it can be intimidating at times.

But, as the marketing rules change, there are some fundamentals that remain constant. To be successful, you will want to do the following, no matter what size business you have:

(1) brand your product

(2) determine who is your target audience

(3) research and learn how to solve their biggest problems

(4) educate about the solutions

(5)  get the sales

(6)  deliver a superior product or service

(7)  create raving fans who will continue doing business with you, and tell them about you

Online marketing is very effective in managing all seven of these rules.

But first, let's look at the broad definition of online marketing to determine exactly what it contains.

## Online Marketing Defined

The definition of online marketing is this: Placing your business or product on the Internet for millions of users to access.  Online marketing is how you use your website to present a product or service in such a way that persuades people to complete some desired action.

That desired action could be anything from clicking a link to subscribe to your mailing list, or clicking on the buy now button to purchase your product.

Once your website is setup and running smoothly, you can use it to guide visitors down the road to purchasing your product. When your site is producing consistent results, you want to keep this engine running. It's just like having a _"Website Marketing Machine"_ that just keeps running and running.

Marketing online also includes creating personalized communications with your customers through the educational content on your website, advertising, and social media. People want to know that you are there ready to respond with useful, and up-to-date information.

One of the great things about online marketing is that you don't need to have a gigantic budget to execute an effective marketing campaign. You can start with very little money, and sometimes, no money at all. Instead of putting up the money, the low-cost methods require an initial investment in time. But at least you can get the ball rolling.

Not only can you save money by using online marketing, but also you can save time by taking advantage of some tools that make online marketing a lot easier. For example, website templates can be used to get your website up and running quickly. Why reinvent the wheel when you can take advantage of templates to get started.

Templates are available for anything we need to create for online marketing. We can use them for creating email newsletters, squeeze pages, shopping carts, and much more. Taking the time to choose the right one for your company will save you time and money.

## What You Need for Online Marketing to be Successful

Having a strong foundation is very important to build a long lasting online marketing platform. These three areas will give you such a foundation.

They are as follows:

### 1. Strong Communication Skills

One of the most important parts of any online marketing is how well you communicate to your potential customers, and your existing ones. The ability to communicate in such a way that persuades people to action is what you want to master.

Much of your online communication is done through your written content, blog posts, emails, and ads. So, it's imperative that you continually learn everything you can to improve your writing skills.

Communication through content writing is a very effective and cost efficient way for you to generate more sales. Most people respond to two-way communication in a very personalized manner. So, communicating effectively through email correspondence, answering blog comments, and educating people about your products helps foster the communication exchange.

And don't forget the magic of consistency. Visitors learn to gain trust in you when you are consistent in your communication efforts. I can't express enough how important consistency is when it comes to building your client base. They will be dependent on you to deliver on your promise, and we can't afford to disappoint.

The more you deliver, the more they will come to trust you. When that trust is developed, your customers will be comfortable knowing that you can deliver.

## 2. Human Resources

If you're going to succeed in the online marketing game, you are going to need people. Even if you are a one-man operation, people are your keys to success.

Who needs to be involved in the online marketing in your organization? Absolutely everyone.

If you are a solopreneur with no employees, you have to turn your existing customers into raving fans who will do marketing for you. The vendors you do business with can be turned into your company advocates that spread the word about you. Everyone that touches your company in any way can be candidates to advocate your business.

## 3. Products People Want To Buy Online

Before you start any marketing online, do the research to be sure that you have a product or service that people want to buy online. Find out what customers are currently buying online to see if you can bring enough value to the table to entice customers to do business with you. Customers will need to find value in what you are selling.

The two benefits that online marketing brings are convenience and cost. Will you be able to demonstrate to potential clients that your services are delivered in a way that's easy to purchase and deliver? Are they willing to pay for that convenience?

What about the cost? Can you deliver the product in a way that makes it cheaper to purchase, as opposed to your competitor? Ask yourself, if customers will find it easier to buy online than finding a local store to purchase it from.

With strong communication skills, people, and viable products or services in place, it is time to turn our attention to establishing online marketing goals to build an action plan around.

## Establishing Online Goals

Establishing online goals is like pouring the cement that will hold your marketing in place until each one is achieved. Goals create the target to aim your marketing efforts toward. Without goals, it is hard to know when you have hit your mark.

All the strategies and tactics we need to execute should be directly driven by the goals we have established. In fact, accomplishing these goals will determine what tactics we need to employ.

Just ensure that our marketing goals coincide with the overall business goals of the company. They are mutually exclusive. The business and online marketing goals must work together to execute the overall company vision.

Although the main goal of any company is to sell products or services, setting marketing goals will allow us to work out just how this selling gets accomplished.

Now let's look at precisely who is going to buy our products.

# Chapter Two: Reaching Your Target Audience

A big factor to successful online marketing is knowing who your target audience is and how to reach them.

## Defining Your Target Market Correctly.

You start by defining your target market. Defining this market is a task that could take volumes to detail every facet, but we can look at our market definition in three major steps.

> **First,** We must look at creating a boundary from which to operate. This boundary of our business can be defined first by a geographic area to be covered.

This "market" is to be segmented into smaller markets. Next, after segmentation, take a detailed look at the way this market operates. How are decisions made about purchasing products and services, what are the requirements for what we call "market demand"? Then gain a full understanding of what that decision making process looks like.

All this must be defined even before we take a look at our ideal customer.

> **Second,** Now that we have our boundaries defined, we must look at exactly how our customers actually behave in the marketplace? What are they spending on? How much of their income is being spent on what products? What are they demanding?

Ask questions like, who are your most valuable clients, and what demographic do they come from? Do they belong to clearly identifiable groups, and how can you reach them?

> **Third,** This stage looks at the reasons behind the behaviors of your potential customers in the marketplace. It answers questions like, "Why are they purchasing the products they buy?" What are the drivers that make them act?

This stage is focused more on the customer's needs. What is it that this particular group in this market segment needs? Finding the "Why" is the very important key to unlocking this part of your plan.

This analysis may not seem like it's that exciting, but answering these important questions will help you define who you will ultimately cater to. Once you have a clear market definition, it's time to look at targeting the exact customers in that market that we can direct our online marketing efforts towards.

## Targeting Our Exact Customer

To determine what types of customers you are trying to reach you should be asking yourself the following questions:

- What age group are you targeting your products?

- Are you selling to males, females, or a specific ethnic group?

- What martial status is appropriate for your product?

- How fast will most Internet connections be?

- What educational level is best?

- Where will customers live?

- Will your customers have any specific hobbies?

- Where do they spend their time?

The biggest advantage of marketing on the Internet is that it allows you to become very targeted towards your desired customers.

## Targeting Different Types of Customers

When you know what type of customers you're targeting, you can concentrate your time, and energy on the marketing that matters most. This type of marketing means you can spend your resources meeting their exact needs.

Your whole marketing communications can be used to speak directly to the needs of that targeted audience.

## Tailor Your Website Your Audience

Your website is the anchor for all your online marketing activities whether you are selling a product or service. Personalizing your website for a specific target audience is something that will keep growing and evolving based on the needs of your target market.

Every bit of content that you use on your site is geared to educate your audience to the fact that you fully understand what their concerns are first and foremost. You understand their journey, their struggles, and what they need.

There is no one size fits all. Whenever you can, use personalization to deepen the experience even more. You don't necessarily need personalized technology to make it happen. The nature of online marketing is perfect for personalization.

Try to limit the number of products or services that you're offering to your customers. "Information overload" is one of the biggest problems on the Internet. If you give your customers too many choices, they'll have a hard time making a decision. The key to avoiding information overload is organization. Also, make sure that products and services are directed towards their specific needs.

Don't make the mistake of thinking that online marketing stops when you generate a sale. Your current customers are the ideal avenue for reaching new customers. You want to get leads from your customers by using marketing concepts such as "tell a friend" emails.

One mistake that many small online businesses make is to focus only on self-promotion. The bottom line is that customers don't care about you. They only care about what you're selling, and what you can do for them.

When someone visits your website, you have about ten seconds to get their attention before they move on to the next website. That means that you have ten seconds to tell this person why they need you.

The homepage of your website should tell people why your service or product is just right for them. Your home page should include information about your company and/or have a personal bio about who you are, but that should not be the main focus.

If you're not sure about whether your website is reaching the right people, ask them. If you provide something of value to people who visit your website, they'll give you good feedback.

Make sure that you let them know they can trust you with the personal information they give you by including a privacy policy on your website that states you won't share any personal information with anyone else. Stick to your policy, and never sell the information to anyone. Otherwise, you'll lose, and abuse their trust.

Once you know the demographics of your customers, you'll know how to spend your marketing budget wisely. You can focus your online promotions using a very targeted marketing strategy. Even though you may end up with fewer people visiting your website, targeted online marketing goes a long way to getting sales from the right people.

# Keyword Research

To place your website in front of the people who want what you offer requires a thorough analysis of the very words people use to find you. These words are called keywords because their ability to find them on the Internet starts there.

Not only is it important to understand your audience, you also want to figure out what search terms they are using to find you. This research begins with a simple brainstorming session to get some general ideas flowing.

Then, a more technical analysis can be done using tools like Google's Adwords to determine which keywords are getting searched the most. These tools also help by giving you ideas for keywords you may not have considered.

Keywords can also be purchased on a pay-per-click basis to increase your visibility in a Google search. Comparing the value of those keywords can indicate their importance to your target audience.

The general rule for keyword research is the broader the term, the harder it is to rank on that keyword. The more specific a keyword, the less competition that keyword receives.

Although we are only scratching the surface of keyword research, this process is one that will give direction to your entire marketing campaigns. The better you get at keyword research, the more visitors you can attract to your site.

If you are not familiar with this skill, or at least know what it is, then study it. It's not that hard to learn and deploy.

## Nothing Replaces Creativity

Nothing gets attention to your website like doing something innovative and creative. People like attention-getters like funny pictures, entertaining videos, and creative new technology. These things help create a buzz about the product or service that you're selling.

If your marketing message contains something strangely unique and entertaining, it is possible that it will get forwarded all around the world.

Come up with your creative marketing message, and test it out on family and friends to see if it is interesting enough to get shared. When that happens, you know that it has the potential to travel the globe.

One important precaution is to always remember that the key to online marketing is to produce quality first. Quality marketing messages that give value are the best route to take. Today online marketing is all about how people react to your website. If they see value in what you're marketing, they will return.

# Chapter Three:  Create Valuable Content

People come to your website for one reason only. They are looking for information. Information that educates, or entertains.  Information that helps them make decisions about their next purchase. Or communicates about what it would be like to make a career change.

Information that helps your visitors find answers to their questions is what is considered valuable.  That type of value is what keeps them coming back to your site.

The Internet is one of the most powerful vehicles of reaching millions of people who need information. It is designed to deliver answers instantly, and provide it just when you need it.

As information changes from day-to-day, your website will change. It will be as dynamic as the needs of the people it serves. When people visit  your site, they are looking for the most up-to-date information.

Website owners who let their sites sit, year after year, without updates can be assured their sites are lost in the black whole of forgetfulness. People see them as stagnant and abandoned. Don't let this be you.

When people visit your site, they want to see fresh content that tells them you are providing relevant information they can use immediately. The assurance of knowing that someone is maintaining the information on your site is what visitors want to feel.

**Update Your Homepage**

The most important page on your site is the homepage. This page is the doorway to everything else on your site. Therefore, making frequent changes to this page is key to keeping your visitors coming back.

Putting the most useful and professional information on your home page is an online marketing strategy that always gets results. If you do nothing else, make updating your homepage a priority.

## What is Good Content?

One of the key ingredients to success on the Internet is creating good website content that Internet users want to read. So, what exactly is considered "good" content.

Content that contains these four key ingredients is what visitors want. If you can produce content that is (1) interesting, (2) factual, (3) well written, and (4) useful, you can be sure that you are producing good content.

### Ingredient #1: Interesting

One of the hardest things to do when it comes to providing good content is making it interesting. Everyone wants our attention these days, and turning information into something that is interesting is the ingredient that will keep visitors glued to your home page.

Interesting content is tied directly to the people for whom the information is most relevant. If they can't relate to what you're saying, no matter how valuable the information is, they won't be interested in it.

So, knowing what your readers want will guide you in determining what information appeals to whom. The more relevant it is to your visitors, the more interesting it will be.

Educating your customers with content that helps them understand your product or service better is what you want.

## Ingredient #2: Factual

The next critical ingredient that web content contains is factual information. People want the facts first. The internet affords the luxury of speed and immediateness, so use it to your advantage by providing the facts as quickly as you can.

Supporting foundational information with examples can be delivered later. But people are looking for the facts. Giving the important factual information up front saves the reader time. Forcing them to dig for the facts is something you want to avoid.

## Ingredient #3: Well Written

Well written web content does not happen overnight. It is a process that starts with an initial idea that gets developed into something that the readers will not only get valuable information from, but will also enjoy reading.

When you start the content development process, you will learn that there will be many improvements that you'll make before you create content that you consider good. That's OK. It's all a part of the process of moving from good to great.

As time goes on, the more feedback you get from the actual users helps you get even more in tune with what they are looking for. Using this feedback keeps you in touch with the issues that are important to them. The more you learn about them, the better you can structure your web content to align with their needs.

In addition, to collecting feedback from your website users, analyzing other websites that hit the top of the search engines can teach you a lot about the information similar websites are providing. These sites are at the top of the search engine results, and to get there, they must be providing information that people are searching for.

Compare what they are offering with the content on your site to see if there are points you would benefit from using. If you do find something to add to your site, make sure your additions get seamlessly added without interrupting your site's natural flow.

The top ranked sites may be using search engine optimization techniques that may be good for search engines, and not necessarily good for the reader. The main point is to meet the needs of the users first.

**Ingredient #4: Valuable**

As mentioned at the beginning of this chapter the more people are able to use your content to help them meet their needs, the more valuable your content becomes.

How do you know what your audience considers valuable? First, you must take the time to do the research to find out exactly who that audience is. Exactly, what do they look like?

Gather everything you can on your target, and put together a profile that looks exactly like your target audience. Then put yourself in their shoes. Ask yourself what can you provide that would be most useful.

Once you determine your target audience, find out how to communicate with them, then ask them directly what it is they want to see. What do they consider important and useful? When you can identify that, and provide it, you are providing real value.

Communication directly to your targeted audience is like speaking to a good friend. They will know that you understand them.

**Creating a Dynamic Home Page**

A dynamic home page is created by constantly publishing content that changes frequently to keep the users interested in what you are offering. With a little bit of thought and creativity, you can get lots of ideas to keep changing your site to keep it fresh.

One idea is to develop five to ten unique versions of your home page and then rotate them every month. This may sound like a lot of work, but one idea for creating dynamic content is to run seasonal promotions. You can create special seasonal messages for holiday specials. These can be fun and bring in a lot of traffic.

Also, if you want to create a more timeless approach, change your site by producing a monthly tips and techniques section. And change it monthly. Create them upfront, and you will have content for the entire year.

## Blog Content

Adding blog content to a website can make your site more dynamic, if you add content on a regular basis. Some sites add blog content on a weekly basis, two times a week, and sometimes every day. This type of content, delivered on a consistent basis, keeps the readers looking forward to new postings.

A blog can keep content available in archives that can be referenced by category or by date.  And unlike a magazine article, it can be accessible whenever you need it.

It may even be a good idea to post an excerpt of your blog posting on your home page. That way your visitors will always have new content to engage.

## Changing your HomePage Too Often

In an attempt to create a dynamic home page, take caution not to change so often that visitors find it hard to navigate.  When people are used to your site, they find comfort in being familiar with it.  They feel as if they know where to go to get the information they are looking for.

If your home page changes too often, you run the risk of confusing them.

Here are a few tips to help as a guideline.  Make sure the headers and navigation on your home page don't ever change.  Change content and images while maintaining the sites original functionality.

Headers and navigation could contain important keywords that are being used to help your search engine optimization. And you don't want to run the risk of compromising your positioning in search engines. Your website will be ranked higher the longer your keywords remain consistent.

You want to find a balance between keeping things on your home page new and exciting, while at the same time, keeping things familiar.

The best way for you to achieve this is to keep the majority of your home page the same, and change only a portion of it frequently. This allows visitors to your website to see new content, and keep your search engine rankings in tact.

**If You Don't Write Content**

If you don't write, or know how to take photographs, there are still some things that you can do to generate content for your website:

- Buy content:  An easy way to add images and photographs that are of high quality is to use a stock photography site. Most of these sites require a monthly subscription, but there are some that don't. You can also just buy the individual images you want.

  Spending a few  dollars on some great images will go a long way in giving your website a professional look. If you are willing to give credit to the photographer, many sites will allow you to download professional images for free.

- Let customers create content:  You can have your customers generate content for your website.  One way to do this is by adding a private social network to your site. This will allow users to add content while communicating with other members on your network.

  Adding a forum is another way to get user content generated. Forums can be set up to allow content by topics or used to answer frequently asked questions.  Another way to create content is by allowing customers to add testimonials to your site telling others how much they like your products or services.

- Links to other content: You can get updated content for your website without having to write it yourself is by pointing your users to related content on other websites. You can provide a link to the original content on another site. Visitors will be appreciative because you are providing them useful information in a convenient way.

## Communication Is Key

We are all bombarded with volumes of messages from companies trying to get our attention. The sheer volume is increasing by the minute. To get someone's attention can be difficult. And keeping it for any length of time is even harder. So, it is important to pay attention to how we are communicating.

People are busy and time is short. So, it is extremely important how we are conveying our marketing message.

The key aspects of good customer communication include the following:

- the ability to read and understand your customers

- the ability to understand which communication style your customers are most likely to respond to, and

- the ability to adapt your website content to the needs of your customers.

When you communicate with your customers, keep your message simple and direct. People don't have a long time to read what you have to say, so make your message fast, and easy to understand.

Here are some basic ideas to keep in mind when writing website content that customers want to read:

- Identify and clarify the marketing message. When you pinpoint your focus, you have the ability to give your customers content that they can trust.

- Gather information. Don't just write website content for the sake of filling up your web space. Research what customers want to read and then write it for them

- Evaluate the information you're writing. Make sure that the information on your website is precise and reliable. Does the information represent the points you want to get across? Is the information fact or opinion? Many times a combination of fact, and customer opinion, go hand in hand.

- Consider the alternatives and implications. Make sure your readers will draw the same conclusions about your web content that you intended to convey when you wrote it. There can be many ways to convey the same message, so make sure that your message is understood by your readers first and foremost.

# Chapter Four: Generating Free Advertising

One way to get your product in front of a lot of people is to use paid ads. This method will increase your reach rather quickly, but has some disadvantages.

The first is that, many times, as soon as your advertising campaign ends, your sales drop considerably. And the second is that paid advertising can get expensive. If you are on a tight budget, this might not be the best route to take. There is another alternative.

One of the best ways to get leads on the Internet is by getting people in search of your product, or service to come to you when they are ready to buy. This process is less intrusive, and will attract visitors who have shown an interest in your offer. The process is called inbound marketing.

## Inbound Marketing

Inbound marketing uses the creation of educational content to attract potential buyers to your product or service. As they consume the content, you move them closer and closer to the purchase of your products. It is a very cost effective way to turn visitors into informed purchasers who will eventually become raving fans of your business.

The content you put on your website is developed to weed out the window shoppers from the serious buyers. It helps you pinpoint more accurately a definite target audience.

Effective inbound marketing is all about putting your product or service in front of potential customers at the exact time that they are looking for it.

Inbound marketing is much different than advertising on radio or television, which are known as "interruptive marketing" techniques. Paid advertising costs a lot more than inbound marketing, and is less effective, because you're attempting to put your product in front of everybody instead of targeting those potential customers who want to find out more about you and your business.

Inbound marketing is the process of sending the right message at the right time, so that it produces the right response.

For example, if you're at the movie theater, and are eating a bag of popcorn. Just when you take a handful of popcorn the Coca-Cola logo appears on the big screen. The next thing you know you're standing in line at the concession waiting to buy a can of Coke.

However, if an advertisement for a new car appears on the big screen while you're watching a movie and eating popcorn, you're less likely to be interested since it's not something you're looking for at that moment.

That kind of interruptive marketing isn't targeted, because it's not something that you are actively looking for. Remember, people who use the Internet are usually looking for information or a solution to a problem. When you put your product in front of them at the right time, you're more likely to reach a real potential customer.

**Search Engine Marketing**

When people want a solution to a certain problem, such as a health issue or taking a vacation, they often look online for the answers, their starting point is usually the search engines. The item they're looking for is typed into the search engine, and the top three items on the search results are usually as far as they get. This is why it's important for you to make sure your company's product or service shows up on the front page.

The art and science getting on the front page of the search engines is called search engine marketing or SEM. Optimizing your website to position you at the top of the search results is called search engine optimization or SEO.

Getting to the top of the search results page can be done by the paid method, or the free method, which is letting your site naturally climb to the top on it's own merit. This is called organic search engine marketing.

Organic search placement takes time, a lot of work, but is the lowest cost. This technique may require a little technical knowledge of HTML, but it is worth the effort to learn. Be prepared to be patient, and work consistently to get the best results.

## Establish Credibility

One of the best ways to attract people to you is to establish credibility as a trusted resource. But, one of the main problems with online marketing is establishing yourself as an authority.

Since there are so many Internet scams out there, people are wary of whom they do business, and even more cautious of companies they are unfamiliar with. As a small business, you need to gain credibility on the Internet by giving users valuable content they can use to make the best purchasing decisions.

The more you provide, the more potential customers will come to rely on you as a trusted resource. And if you can't provide the right information, then point them to other sites that can.

Your recommendations mean a lot because you are looking out for their best interest. You become a trusted professional, when you provide information that actually solves their problems.

## Share Content On Other Websites

Another way that you can build credibility online is to swap content with other credible websites. If you can position an article that includes a link to your website, especially with another site that is already at the top of their field, you increase your chances of gaining more credibility.

Writing articles that contain valuable information that others want to share can get you some great leads. When a potential customer reads your article, and gets helpful information, you establish yourself as an expert in your field quickly. When the prospect links over to your website, you have a very good lead that you can turn into sales.

People who use the Internet want immediate results. They know exactly what they are looking for, so your advertising message needs to be appropriate, concise, and to the point. You need to think about what kind of people will be accessing the website, and where you plan to post your article on that site.

## Referral Marketing

One of the most common ways that people find new websites is through referral marketing. In fact, some businesses get the majority of their work that way.

Getting a referral is like getting a vote of confidence from a trusted source. And sometimes, that's all you need to get your foot in the door. Once you are there, it's up to you to execute.

If you are doing the type of work that people are delighted with, there is a good chance that your customers will tell someone else about you. Then, they tell someone else, and the next thing you know, word starts spreading about your business.

It's a good idea to ask your customers to give you a written testimonial that you can post on your website. Prospective customers really read those testimonials when making the decision to use you. Make sure that the testimonials are strictly voluntary. Paid testimonials are not acceptable.

## Viral Marketing

Viral marketing works in much the same way as referral marketing, except viral marketing spreads like a wild fire reaching people all over the globe. You've probably seen this in action when someone posts a funny video on the Internet. They tend to get shared very quickly.

Viral marketing takes advantage of the socialization needs of society. No matter how small the social network starts out, effective viral marketing can turn a small unknown company into an online sensation. Some of the biggest companies on the Internet rely on viral marketing to stay successful.

## Email Marketing

If you are not already using this, a simple strategy to get your marketing message out there is to use your email signature as a marketing vehicle. It usually contains information that identifies the sender. The name and address of the sender is what most people use the email signature for, but with some marketing creativity, it can be turned into free advertising.

The best part is that it's free, and you can start using it right away. There is absolutely no cost to set up. Just simply create the message you want to convey, and it gets attached to every message you send.

There is no waiting involved in this process. You can start today and start realizing results immediately. You want your readers to leave with a parting thought. What better way to give that message than with your email signature?

## Free, Free, Free - Something for Free

Who doesn't want to get something for free these days? There's no better way to get people talking about your company. When you offer something that is free the word spreads quickly.

Free offers will always bring traffic to your website. All that traffic may not convert into sales, but some will. It's the traffic that converts that will end up being your potential customers.

There are expenses involved with a giveaway that small online businesses may not be able to afford. But that's when your creativity can kick in to brainstorm low cost offerings. Creating a free digital product can be a great alternative.

You can save by giving your free gift away to a limited number of people who buy a product from you. For example, give away tickets to the first 20 customers who buy a certain product from you. This method encourages sales and minimizes your expenses at the same time.

Using email as a marketing strategy makes it easy for people to spread the word about you to others anywhere in the world.  If you can create infectiously engaging emails, they can generate a buzz around you and your product or service.

Soon, your potential customers will begin to recognize your logo or company name.  Continually providing them with quality email content is the way to gain trust, credibility, and to close a sale.

Domain Names:  One very important part of any effective marketing strategy that will help get the word out about you is selecting the right domain name. Here are some key points to remember.

Choosing a memorable domain name is probably one of the best ways to help people find and keep returning to your website. There are a few things you can do to make that name as memorable as possible.

First, keep the name as short as possible. Shorter names are not only easier to remember, but also take very little time to type. Avoid using hyphens or dashes in your name. The simpler the better.

The spelling of your domain name helps make your name memorable. If it's easy to spell, visitors should have no problem finding you. Also, picking a name that relates to what you're selling can help make your name easier to remember.

The last thing to remember is to choose a domain name that is based on a keyword that people use to search. Thinking like a customer who wants to find you on the web, you can ask what would they type into the search engine to find your product or service. Using that word as a part of your domain name can help them find you faster, and helps your site show up in their search results.

You want to pick a domain name that is easy to remember, easy to spell, and that relates to what you're selling. When people easily find your website you'll want to make sure that your home page content is dynamic so they keep returning to get the latest content.

# Chapter Five: Email Marketing

There is a big question about whether or not email is still an effective way to reach customers. Many people think that using social media, search engine marketing, and content marketing has diminished its effectiveness.

If we approach all of our marketing channels as more of an integrated front instead of seperate marketing solos, email can be effectively integrated into each one. No one marketing approach can stand on its own.

The effectiveness of email is that it can reach people directly with very personalized messages that can directly target the needs of the potential customer.

When done well, email marketing can meet the needs of your customers and increase your brand awareness. Most customers prefer email over any other type of selling.

Email is still the number one activity online, which makes it a great online marketing tool now and long into the future.

## Permission Based Email

One important key that separates an effective email marketing strategy from just becoming annoying marketing spam is to only focus on permission based mail. This means that customers need to give you permission to receive mail from you. This is known as 'opt in " or permission based email.

The days of renting or buying an email are long gone. When you send email to people without their permission, it is considered spam. Spam will quickly give your company a bad name, and will take away any trust that customers have in you.

Building your own list of opt in emails is the best way to get quality leads from people who want to hear from you. Servicing a list like that will tremendously build better business relationships that will ultimately benefit you and your customers.

Using permission based email marketing allows you to give your customers exactly what they want. At the same time, it allows you to communicate with your customers to help find out exactly what they need. As you fulfill their needs, you establish the base of a relationship that builds long term customer loyalty.

## Build Your Email List

Building an email list takes time and effort, but once you do, you'll have the names of people who are genuinely interested in what you're selling.

To get people to join your email list, potential customers need to see the value in joining. This value is the information you provide that solves their problems or makes their life easier.

For example, if people on your list need more information to help them make a smart purchase, you may want to provide product reviews. Or provide a checklist of things they need to know before making their purchase.

Trust is the other ingredient that will help with your email signups. You need to gain trust before asking people to give their information. As you provide value, they will more likely want to join your list to return the favor.

Knowing you keep their information private is another way to gain their trust. Let your customers know that you value their trust and respect their privacy by posting a privacy policy on your website. People need to understand that you will not sell their information.

To build your list, the best place to start is to ask for a name and email address. That is it. You don't want to ask for too much information at first. The more information you ask at one time turns people off. Keep it short.

As time goes on, your future marketing efforts will uncover other information that you need to continue your marketing efforts. Eventually, you can begin to start a dialog where you can ask questions to help target exactly what they want and need.

Another way to gain their confidence is to tell them what you'll be emailing them first. Then make sure you deliver exactly what you said. That way customers know what to expect, and when you deliver as promised, it's the best way to gain their trust.

A quick caution, if you do any joint promotion with another online company or any influencer, don't give away your email list.

All emails to people on your list should come directly from you. You can include the name of the person or company you're cross promoting in your newsletter, but make sure they can't email the people on your list directly.

You'll lose your customer's trust if they think you've sold their personal information. Even the slightest indication that this is happening will cause them to unsubscribe from your list forever.

Attending trade shows and networking events is another great way to add names to your email list. You can collect business cards and if they contain an email address, go ahead and add them to your list. Always provide a way for them to unsubscribe.

A good rule of thumb is: if someone gives you their business card that has their email address on it you can safely assume that it's okay to send them an email at least once. They will alway have the option to unsubscribe.

Building an email list of interested prospects is a great way to directly reach your customers in a personalized way. This will be one of your biggest assets.

## Goal Oriented Marketing

Once you've created your email list, it's time to develop an email marketing plan to turn those prospects into customers. For most people the goal is to make sales, however, you may want to develop a plan to move them to the next phase of their buyer's journey instead.

The benefits of defining your marketing goals are many, and once you get started, you'll find that you'll want to use goals for more than just marketing.

Every business is different, so the goals you set will be particular to what you want to achieve. Determine your goals and put a plan in place to accomplish those goals. Breaking those goals into actionable steps will lead to their accomplishment.

Also, setting goals will give you an opportunity to track your progress. The more quantifiable the goals are, the more accurately you can measure them. This measuring stick will help you make the changes necessary to keep on track.

## Email Newsletters

Email newsletters are a great way to communicate information about you and your company with your email list. Even though you have great content on the homepage of your website, and on your blog, having a newsletter can add even more to the user experience.

In order to get subscribers to your newsletter, consider providing some incentives for people who sign up. Again, it's trading value for value. If you can find out what your customers want, you can offer it in your newsletter. Here are some ideas to get you started.

Ideas for Content:  You don't always have to offer discounts or a free product as incentives to customers, although these are very enticing.  The content of the newsletter itself can be a good incentive.

Good newsletter content includes:

- Customers submitted success stories.

- Information from industry experts in your field.

- A section for frequently asked questions.

- Interesting news and/or statistics about your industry.

- Testimonials from customers.

- Tips for using your products or services.

Good newsletter content is anything that catches the interest of your customers. They particularly want to know what's in it for them.

A newsletter, just like your homepage, has only a few seconds to attract the attention of your customer before they decide to delete it. Your newsletter should immediately let your customer know what you can do for them, how you're going to do it, and why they should do business with you.

Newsletters are a great way to create brand awareness but make sure that you take into consideration the content, the length, and the frequency of the newsletter.

Keep it Short: Your newsletter should be concise, short, and get to the point. It should be no more than 1200 words and deal with no more than five different products or services at one time. People don't like to read lengthy emails.

This could be a roadblock to you sending out newsletters on a regular basis. If there is too much information in the first email your customers won't want to click through to your website.

The ability to track email gives you the ability to see what is working and what changes you need to make to get the click throughs to your website or for your offers.

When you provide too much information in your newsletter, people will not click through to your site. And a no-click means you have no way to convert that click into a potential sale.

Keep your newsletters short and provide opportunities to get more information by giving links to your site.

Frequency and Timing: The question is, how often should I send out my newsletter and what time would get the best results? You need to determine when and how often you're going to send out email newsletters. You don't want to send emails out too often. This will overwhelm your customers. But, you don't want to wait too long between emails or your customers will forget about you.

Timing and consistency will vary depending on what type of business you have. A general rule of thumb is to send no more than once a week, and no less than once a month. The Direct Marketing Association's National Client Email reports that 35 percent of marketers send two to three emails a month.

Others report that Tuesdays and Thursdays tend to be best for sending emails which have an overall higher open rate. You can send on Mondays and Wednesdays, but the open rate may not be as high.

The best time to send is between 10 and 11am. But if you really want to know what your customers prefer, just ask them. When they join your list, just ask how often they would like to receive emails from you.

Finally, it may be good to track your emails statistics to see what times are best for your audience.

## Autoresponder Services

What exactly is an autoresponder service? An autoresponder is a service that allows you to automatically send out emails to a group, or several groups. These groups are called subscribers because they actually give you permission to send them emails.

Autoresponder services allow you to write emails, schedule, and track it's performance. Once it's all set up, the emails can be sent automatically. These services take the manual work out of maintaining your email database.

To save even more time producing your newsletter, these services have templates available to modify and use. This means you don't have to spend time learning html to create a professional looking newsletter.

If you use the templates, make sure you choose one that fits well with your existing branding to keep continuity between all your marketing channels. Consistency is the key to effective online marketing.

Tracking your campaign progress makes managing a lot easier. With it comes the ability to receive reports on things like open rates, click through rates, what devices were used, and who are the top clients with the highest open rates.

This information lets you change the content of your newsletter when you know what it is that your customers most want to read. As you start to send out more newsletters you'll get a better feel for what your customers want.

Autoresponder services allow you to create subscription signup forms that you can place on your website, blog, or a landing page. With this ability, you can target the people based on what they are interested in. Then you can create targeted lists and create a newsletter with information for people on each list.

If your newsletter contains enough value, your customers are more likely to forward the email on to friends and family. This expands your reach even further.

Remember, no matter how great your newsletter is, there is no guarantee that people will read it. But there is one way that you can make sure your newsletter isn't deleted before it's read. That is to make a compelling subject line.

## Enticing Subject Lines

When people get an email, the first thing they do is see who it's from and the next thing is to see what they want. All this takes place a few seconds. That's how long it takes to make a decision to read or not.

The subject line is what they scan to decide whether to open it or not. Therefore, the subject has to be compelling. It has to be short but also say the very things that make a reader want to take action.

Here are some simple rules for creating a great subject line:

- Keep the subject line between five and ten words. Make it direct and short. Even though it's short, make it impactful. Subject lines usually get truncated depending on the device you're using to read it. Use strong and descriptive words with clear messages.

- Emphasize the benefits to the reader. Remember, readers want to know what's in it for them. The word "reward" is just enough to get their attention. A reward can be information or a discount coupon, or a free download. The key is to entice your customers to want to read more and open the email.

- Ask questions. Putting a question in the subject line causes a reader to become curious and want to know more. When you ask the right question, the email sounds more like it's coming from a colleague rather than a stranger.

- Personal subject lines. One big mistake that screams "spam" is sending your email to "undisclosed recipients". You can personalize your email with a specific first name or email address. And make sure the sender has your name or your company's name.

- Take advantage of holidays and current events. If there is an upcoming holiday, such as Christmas, you can tie that into your subject line. For example, "Save money on your Christmas Shopping".

- Avoid using the word "free". Hard sales phrases, such as "free" and "limited offer", are often filtered out by email services since they are a clear indication of spam. As well, try to avoid using hype which includes explanation marks or all capital letters.

# Chapter Six:  Build a Community Online

Over 84% of Internet users take part in some type of online community.  We call them "Cyber Groupies".  And 79% of Cyber Groupies participate in one particular group where they stay in contact regularly.  But just why are online communities such a draw for so many people?

- Online communities are much like a virtual gathering place for people to get together with people with similar interests.

- Online communities are a great place to learn something new.

- Online communities are where people can be anonymous and share their problems and fears.

- Online communities allow companies to get suggestions for product improvements

- Online communities allow people to get support with their problems from other people in the group who have experiences they want to share

Online Community Defined: An online community can be accessed anywhere at any time. Some of the components of an online community include chats, message boards, newsletters, event calendars, and anything else that lets an Internet user interact with others who are online.

Is it necessary to be concerned about online communities for your online marketing strategy? Customers who take part in an online community are a good target for your sales because they have a high affinity for loyalty to your product when they are participating in your online community.

If you can build a strong and solid online customer community, you know that you've built a loyal following for your company. These loyal customers will share news of your company online which will further increase your sales.

Message Boards:  A lot of companies and organizations benefit from  providing their customers and members a message board on their website.  They can break message boards up into categories for different products or services, and encourage customers to share their ideas and opinions with each other.

This is the first step towards building an online community.  Customers who join will answer each other's questions, thereby saving time and  money on customer service.

These boards do require a moderator to keep information on the forum accurate. Also, moderators can identify abusers of the board and discontinue their membership if necessary.

Message boards can also be used to collect some great feedback about the products or services you're selling. Obtaining honest feedback from customers lets you better take care of their needs.

Message boards can be an important part of your website marketing strategy. Setting one up can even be done without spending a lot of time and money. Begin by asking your website hosting company if they can provide you with a message board template as a part of your hosting package. Otherwise look on the Internet for a free one. You will save money with a free one but it may take more time to set it up on your own.

Choose a message board that fits the look and feel of your website so that you're maintaining consistency.

Message Board Content: The content that your community is built around will determine how successful your online community is. If your site is a professional one with quality content, you are on your way. Always keep in mind that it's content that attracts readers and should be your major concern when it comes to your decision to develop an online community.

Your customers can help keep your content fresh with content ideas that will keep your online community interesting. You'll learn exactly what your customers are looking for and just how you can provide that information to them.

Message Board Calendar:  To allow people to meet offline, calendars are a vital part of the online community. Your company can post events offline with all the information people need to find out how to attend.

If your company doesn't have any offline events, you can still use the calendar to post information about events within your industry that others in your community may want to attend.

Contests:  You can use contests as a way to get customers excited about your company and your website. You can give a prize to the person who has the best story about how your product has benefited them.  When the contest is over you can post these stories, along with the names of the winners, on your website.  This conveniently provides you with customer testimonials and gives you insight into your customers' interests.

Maintaining an Online Community:  Maintaining your online community can take a lot of work in the beginning.  You'll need to invest a certain amount of time and effort to get it set up correctly with the appropriate topics you want to discuss.

Once it is set up, moderating the discussions will take time. Emails responses must be given as quickly as possible to show that your community is active. But after awhile you can delegate some of these responsibilities to other members of the group.

When your online community is in its beginning stages you might have to plant some of your own questions, answers, and comments to the message board.

Eventually, once traffic builds, it will start to flow on its own and will require less maintenance.

# Chapter Seven: Strategies for Affiliate Marketing

Affiliate marketing can be a little confusing until you understand how it works. An Internet user clicks on a link on your website and is taken to a web page that has been referred to them by the website owner. If they make a purchase from the referral, the link supplier gets a commission from the sale.

When it comes to affiliate marketing you need to choose partnerships that have something in common with the product or service that you're selling. Or you need to be recommending a product or service that you currently use.

Affiliate marketing can be very cost effective, particularly for small online businesses. However, if you choose the wrong affiliate, or too many affiliate partners, it might be more harmful. It's the trust factor again. If you refer people to products that they have a bad experience with, it could reflect badly on you.

## Adding Affiliate Partners To Your Website

As a small business you need to be cautious with your marketing budget. A larger portion of your budget should go to promoting our own products. However, affiliate marketing can allow you to use the power of the affiliate partners brand to minimize your marketing expense.

When you add an affiliate partner to your website, you need to ensure that you're going to see positive results from the union. These results can include more traffic to your website, increased online sales, or more satisfaction from your customers.

Affiliate marketing works best when both you and your partner company each provide a related service or product to the same types of customers.

Powerful affiliate marketing: Studies show that most online users like the idea of affiliate marketing because it helps them to make decisions about the hundreds of brand name products that they come into contact with on the Internet. Sometimes there are so many to choose from that a referral from someone they trust help makes their buying decision that much easier.

Affiliate partnerships need to make sense and customers need to understand the connection for it to be a win-win.

<u>Guidelines for affiliate marketing</u>: If you have the right affiliate partners you can get plenty of marketing collateral as well. This saves you time and the cost of creating it yourself. Working with affiliates can also give you access to a larger customer base.

Following are some important affiliate marketing guidelines:

- What is your affiliate partner's appeal to your customers? Will it make your customers feel better about using their products?

- What do you and your affiliate partner have in common? Are both of your products innovative? Are they dependable and reliable?

You want to make sure that your product offerings make sense for your current customer base. You don't want to lose your current customer base but instead, you want to increase it.

- How does your affiliate marketing partnership benefit your customers? Will it save them money? Or will it save them time?

  Your marketing campaign should focus on making the benefits crystal clear to your customers.

- Your goal with affiliate marketing should be to find the best solutions for your customers even if you don't produce what they're looking for.

- Will your customers easily be able understand why you recommend this partner, and quickly see the connection and value of your partnership?

- Does the affiliate marketing partnership bring you into contact with new customers? Will your customer base broaden by offering the affiliate partners' products?

The above guidelines need to be answered before you join an affiliate's marketing program. These marketing promotions take a great deal of time and energy to be executed correctly. However, when done well, selling an affiliate's product can bring you results that are far better than other online marketing methods.

One of the basic rules of any online marketing is: bring customers to your website by offering valuable solutions to their problems, even if you have to recommend other companies' products. Your message, content, and promotions should be focused on the customer first.

## Integrating Partnership Products

When it comes to affiliate marketing partnerships, you need to incorporate the benefits of the products you are recommending into the overall design of your marketing campaigns. This way your customers will understand the connection between both products or services, and why they will benefit them.

Simply putting a link from your website to another company's website is not enough. It's never a good idea to leave your customers wondering why you want them to link to another site or use another company's products. They want to know where they are going and why. This knowledge just helps improve a customer's shopping experience by helping them make informed buying decisions.

You'll want to incorporate content from your affiliate partner's website so that you both can expand your reach. However, you'll need to incorporate this content into your website seamlessly so that it flows naturally. As a result, you maintain a professional appearance that builds the customers trust and confidence.

Keep Your Marketing Goals In Mind: Always keep your business goals in mind no matter what online marketing strategy you use. This means that all your website content, promotions, and activities with your affiliate marketing partners encourages your customers to find the exact solutions they are looking for, no matter where they are in their buyer's journey.

The more helpful you are in providing the answers they need, the more likely they will buy from you. Remember, customers are looking for solutions.

# Chapter Eight: SEO - Rising to the Top of Search Engines

If users are looking for your business, the most common way for people to access your website is through search engines. This means you have to be on the first page. If your company is on that first page, you will capture free traffic which can amount to free advertising.

This means that your company website needs to be found at the top of the Internet search engines, or at least on the first page, no matter if they use Google, Yahoo, Bing or any other popular search tool.

Getting to the top of the search page takes time and hard work. You have to keep up with search technology and implement those methods to keep your site on top.

However, if your website is well designed, search engines can be your best ally in generating more free Internet traffic.

## What Is Search Engine Optimization?

Search engine optimization, or SEO, is the process of increasing the quality and quantity of website traffic by increasing the visibility of a website or a web page to users of a web search engine.

SEO in particular refers to the improvement of unpaid results and excludes direct traffic/visitors, and the purchase of paid placement.

It is the practice of using the techniques to place your website so that its visibility ranking increases in search engine databases. You want your website to have a high ranking and be seen as relevant to a user's search.

Successful SEO websites use keywords (terms that people use to search for an item) and articles based on those keywords to make their sites visible when people search for those terms. Those same keywords are used in strategic places on your website.

As you are building your website, using those keywords effectively throughout your website content is key. These keywords can go in certain places within your html coding for each webpage. This will increase the likelihood that the search engines will find those pages and rank them higher in the search engine database.

Before you submit your website to the most popular search engines you'll want to make sure that you're making the most of optimized keywords, as discussed in Chapter 2. The quality of your website is a big factor in ranking your website in the search engine database.

The more you understand the importance of keywords usage and placement in your content, the better chance you'll have in making sure you use that best marketing tactic to keep you climbing up the search engines.

**Optimizing your Website**

Optimizing your website is the process of making changes to your website so that it will appear higher in the search engine results pages.

The more relevance the search engines determine your website has for a given search, the higher that website will rank.

One of the most important things for you to remember when you're optimizing your website for search engines is that these engines read text and ignore graphics. This means that you need to focus on the text that is part of your website content. Although the graphic is ignored the meta data around the graphic is relevant. But the key is text. So let's talk about how we can optimize the text to improve your ranking.

The Right Keywords: All keywords are not the same in that some keywords are searched more than others. The ones that are searched the most are the ones that you want to optimize your site around. The more people are searching for that keyword, the more visitors will find your site if it is on the first page of the search engine results.

Before you start optimizing, doing some keyword research will reveal the right keywords for your business. There are many ways to do the research and many programs that will make this easier. Some are paid but others are free. Google has their own tool called Adwords that can be used.

Once your target keywords are identified, you can begin to optimize your pages based on these targeted keywords.

Text on your Home Page: Once you've decided which keywords are best for optimizing your website you'll want to put those keywords into strategic places in the content of your website.

You'll want to start by focusing on the page titles and move onto the first paragraph on your homepage. It's the first thing that most search engines read to determine if your website is relevant to a user's search. In that first paragraph you'll want to use your keywords in the first sentence, preferably, the first word in the first sentence.

Keeping a natural flow of user understandable text, you can use the keyword throughout the content. Be careful not to over use them because Google will think you are spamming the system and will ban your site.

<u>Using HTML Tags</u>: You'll need to make sure that you use your keyword in with the right tags in your HTML code. These tags include the title tag, meta description, and the Alt tag. They are the ones to focus on first.

These optimizations are called on page SEO because they relate directly to coding of the content on each page of your site. Off page optimization refers to things not directly related to the content of the pages. They include things like link building and social media.

## Submitting Your Website to Search Engines

Registration with search engines, such as MSN, Yahoo, and Google, is something you can do to help get your site listed. Before you decide what search engines to submit to, you should do a careful study of what features each engine provides.

Some of the features that you should be focused on include (1) how they promote websites, (2) what they offer in regards to advertising, and (3) if they have any other resources available. There are analyzers available on the Internet that will help you compare search engines.

There are a few important things that you should focus on when it comes to submitting your website to the right search engine. This includes:

- The search engine generator should provide you with automatic updates.

- The registration process should allow you to include the purpose of your business and website.

- Do a quick study to find out where other businesses in your industry are submitting their website.

Your main goal should be to submit your website to as many top search engines as you can so that you get the maximum exposure. This will allow your customers and potential customers to find you fast and easily.

Search engine spiders: A search engine spider, also known as a web crawler, is an Internet bot that crawls websites and stores information for the search engine to index. It's an ongoing process due to the fact that there are new web pages created every minute.

These search engines use sophisticated algorithms to determine who gets ranked higher. When your website matches the keyword searched, Google wants to deliver the most relevant results. That is where your keywords come in. The more keywords on your site that match, the more visibility your page gets.

When you overuse keywords and key phrases you risk being noticed by search engine spiders as keyword abuse. If that happens, they bypass your web pages for inclusion into the search engine, period. Do you want to risk being left out of search engines by being guilty of keyword abuse?

Using a high keyword density may seem like a good idea when you first start developing web content for your website but the hazards far outweigh the risks. Be watchful and play by the rules.

<u>Goals for Successful Websites</u>:  One of the main goals for having a business on the Internet is to avail the company to potential customers all over the world. But not everyone is an ideal client. The Internet gives you a way to target just the right customer who is looking for your product.

Those are the ones you want to build your business. You want to have as many qualified customers and potential customers on your list as you can.

So the goal of your website should be to attract those potential customers with engaging information that makes people want to do business with you. If you can use your website to turn those people into paying customers, your site becomes one of your biggest assets.

Once you've built up a list of customers, you'll want to make sure that they do repeat business with you.  Repeat sales are the backbone of a successful business. One of the ways that you can achieve repeat sales is by generating great communication through your website. You can accomplish this good communication by using the following:

- Affiliate programs

- Coupons and bonuses for repeat customers

- Contests

- Newsletters that provide valuable information about what they're looking to purchase

- Discussion groups and forums

- Pleasant relationships with your associates

- Chat available on your site

As mentioned previously you'll already have a lot of customer information that you can use.  This includes data that you've collected from previous sales, communication with your customers, and targeted email opt-in lists.

You'll also want to collect as much customer information that aids in retaining them.  But just how do you go about gathering that data? There are several different techniques that you can use to get the data that you need.

The most important thing to remember is always be honest when you're getting information from your customers. If you use deceptive means to get the data you risk losing their trust. If being honest and above board means that you lose some of those opportunities, the pay off will be the trust and respect you earn.

Consistently doing what you say you will do will alway gain their trust. Asking anyone voluntarily to provide you with certain types of information carries the responsibility to keep that information private and safe.

The following are methods of collecting customer data that will help you keep track of sales and profit. This customer data can be found in the following places:

- customer order forms

- warranty card information

- servicing information

- records of returned products

- questionnaires filled out at time of purchase

The above information is very helpful but you'll need a bit more to build up a successful database that contains a wide-range of customer information.

The Internet has provided you with some great opportunities to use the latest tools to your advantage, such as CRMs, customer relationship management systems, lead pages, and sales funnels.

All this technology means that you can use some very appealing and winning methods for having your customers leave you the information that you need.

Once you've got their interest, there are many ways that you can correspond with them:

- weekly newsletters

- automated emails, targeting one time customers, referrals, and repeat customers

- discount or free product offers

- groups and forums

- follow up phone calls

- social media

- snail mail

Corresponding with your customers is much simpler after you've profiled them, and know what they want to see and hear.

# Chapter Nine: Building Email Lists

The Direct Marketing Association reports that on average they see a 430 percent return on investment (ROI) for businesses in the US that use email marketing as a part of their marketing strategy. This is because email subscribers that join your email list from your website by double-opting in, are extremely interested in what you have to offer. This is why they convert so well into paying customers.

**Importance of Building Lists**

One of the most important rules aspects of online marketing is the need to have an opt-in email list. The larger your list, the more successful your online business will be. The bottom line is, if you want to have a successful online business you need to have an active email list.

Many online businesses don't realize the benefits of an

opt-in list besides the bottom line of profit. Each time someone buys something from you, you need to make the effort to get their email address. Missing this opportunity will cause you to lose all chances of future communication with them.

Online marketing studies show that successful online businesses think of their opt-in emailing list as their most valuable asset. They religiously backup their email list so that there is no chance of losing it. Without it you would lose valuable customer communications which is the backbone of any online business success.

The more extensive your email opt-in list is the more sales opportunities you get. When you regularly stay in touch with your customers, you can be sure that a percentage will return to your website to make a purchase, or return for a repeat purchase.

Make sure that your online website has opt-in options on every web page. This way people who read your website have every opportunity to give you their email address for future contact with your company.

Email has the touch of personal communication, if done right, that will give you the advantages of giving valuable information to your subscribers, but will also allow you to receive communications back from them.

This interaction not only allows you to collect very viable marketing information, but also allows you to build a level of trust that makes it easier for them to want to do business with you.

Once your email interactions get started, continue to communicate until they unsubscribe. The more you interact, the more you will increase your sales.

Opt-in Lists: An opt-in list is a list of people who have given you permission to receive more information from you. This information can be emails that contain your newsletter, special promotions, blog notifications, and more.

How do you develop your opt-in email list? There are many ways to go about building an email list, but one way is to use your website as a marketing tool.

Email signup forms can be placed on your website to allow people to sign up to your list. These forms can be created in an email autoresponder and published on your website.

Opt-in forms can be constructed from templates that make it easy for you to modify to reflect your personal branding. They look professional and saves you time.

The following are some ideas for content you can send:

- Newsletters: Newsletters contain information about the product or service you're selling, or information about new products. We introduced these in Chapter 5.

- Blog Post Notifications: Notification for newly created blog posts can be sent to your email subscribers.

- Discount and Bonuses: Special discounts and bonuses can be sent to your list for purchasing future products.

- Product Launches and Presales: Presales are a great way to gage the success of a future product, or service. Products that are developed can be launched to this list first before rolling it out to the public.

- Surveys: Surveys can be sent to collect feedback on how well you are doing. This a great way to get first hand feedback from your subscribers

Always remind people why they are receiving emails from you, and make sure they alway have the option to unsubscribe.  This way they don't think that they are being spammed.

When people have the option to unsubscribe, they feel as though they are in control.

# Chapter Ten:  Forget about SEO

Forget about SEO, at least for a minute, long enough to concentrate on your image. Many Internet websites rely so much on pleasing the search engines that they forget that being recognizable is just as powerful.

Your content is created for your customers first and search engines second. And as soon as your customers reach your site, they want to experience something that they want to remember. That's where good branding comes into play.

## Successful Branding

Successful branding is all about recognition from not only your customers, but also with anyone who comes in contact with you and your business.

When your customers can recognize your product or service, and differentiate you from your competition, that is the first step in your branding. There are several methods to ensure your name is out there and that your customers recognize you immediately.

No matter what, creating a clear straight forward branding package requires a clear strong message. This message is an expression of your style, and combines your values with that style.

This style can not only be communicated in the visual aesthetic of your website, but also expressed in all your communication from content to advertising.

The following are considerations to create the branding for your website:

- Visual communication.  Your visual communications can start with your company logo. Create a company logo which displays your message in a creatively attractive way. Then, use it on all your customer communications.  This includes brochures, business cards, catalogues, stationary letterheads, and any other marketing media.

- Creative packaging. If you sell products, creativity can be the key to getting noticed. Develop creative packaging for your products that stand out and get noticed. For digital products presentation is everything. Apply the same principles to them.

- Beneficial Ad Campaigns. While you are spending money trying to get customers, also take advantage of the opportunity to promote your brand. Any media exposure to promote that brand will boost public awareness of you and your company.

Branding can be powerful yet simple. Sometimes that simple message can be remembered for a long time. What matters is that your audience can grasp and resonate with it.

A simple strategy for getting started with successful branding includes:

- Developing a strong mission statement. Know exactly where your company is going and how you want to get there with a strong mission statement.

- Defining company goals. Defining company goals bring clarity to what you are going to accomplish with your marketing and branding.

- Identifying your ideal customers. Branding is all about identifying your customers and matching their values with your.

- Selecting the right marketing tactics. The methods of marketing can identify your company brand. Picking the right marketing helps build that brand you want to portray. Customers like reliability and simplicity which can be qualities your brand is built around.

The end result of successful branding creates products and services that are positively identified because your company understands its customer's values, and centers its existence around those positive principles.

When done right, this positive recognition called branding is what will develop a strong company image that customers want to identify with, and buy products from.

## Market Research

One of the most important things any business owner can do is market research. Find the market and position yourself right in the middle of it, and you will have plenty of sales.

A quick definition is the process of finding out how viable your product or service is and looking at the prospective customer base that needs what you offer.

You want to know what they are buying, where they are getting their product information, who are they currently doing business with. How would they react to new trends in the industry, and what will they do as new companies enter the existing market. How will you get them to buy from you, is another key question.

The only way to get answers to these questions is to conduct your own market research.

## Firsthand Exploratory Research

When you watch and listen to what your customers are concerned with, you are more likely to zero in on exactly what they want from your products and services. However, talking with them, directly, will reveal even more. This exploration can prove to uncover what you should do to satisfy their needs.

To conduct this type of exploration, the best source of information comes from talking directly to the customer. This type of communication gives you a first hand glimpse into their emotional side of the buying process. Many times you will find that they're ready and willing to discuss their experiences with you.

Asking about the problems they are having, and finding out what can be done to solve them is what you can learn through your discussions.

If you can't meet them first hand, surveys will be the next best option. It may be challenging to convince some people to fill out a survey, but providing some type of compensation would be helpful.

## Secondhand Research

Secondhand research through public sources like government agencies is another option. Two of the most common sources of government information are the U.S. Census Bureau and the Bureau of Labor & Statistics. Both will let you look up information for free.

Other commercial organizations like the Gartner Group and Forrester give insights into specific industries, and report on marketing information. These reports are not free, and are available to be downloaded.

## Continuous Market Research

Marketing research is not a one-time event. It will be good to conduct it on an ongoing basis. Markets change rapidly and new problems develop everyday. Continuous marketing research will keep you on top of any changing conditions.

The steps involved are the following:

## Step 1. Know Your Ideal Customer and Build Some Personas

When it comes to getting customers, understanding who they are will help you assist them at every stage of their buying journey. Therefore, collecting this type of customer data can be arranged into a customer persona.

A persona is a fictional representation of your ideal customer used to help visualize your audience by targeting your communications specifically for them.

What does a persona contain? Information such as age, gender, geographic location, job title(s), income, family size, challenges, aspirations are some places to start.

Some people not only write down this information, but also create a character to visualize that person making it easier to direct your communication toward.

## Step 2. Choose A Segment of Those Persona and Engage With Them

Now that you've created your personas, it's time to actually engage with them to solicit feedback to learn more about them.

Speaking directly with them may be a possibility. The ones closest to the buying experience are the ones who have recently made a purchase. They will be able to speak clearly about their purchase, and what worked or didn't work for them.

In some cases a survey would be a better means of communication especially if most of your sales are online. Leaving room for plenty of open ended questions will give the customer plenty of opportunity to freely express what they think.

Another option would be to organize small focus groups, which can bring a variety of personality types to interview. Whichever communication vehicle you choose, open, honest discussion will get you very valuable information to build your marketing around.

## Step 3. Recruit a Sample Survey Group

Choosing a specific cross sampling of your customer database to study gives you the opportunity to get a better perspective of your customer base.

This sample can include people who have recently made a purchase, those you expressed an interest but didn't buy, potential customers that experienced a problem, and those who were not interested at all.

You are hand picking, so you can choose from a wide spectrum.

Include people from social networks you've engaged with, and people from your personal network. These could be friends, neighbors, and co-workers.

Make sure you provide an incentive for them to participate. This study could take 30-50 minutes. So, reward them with a discount card, or exclusive content that is helpful to them.

## Step 4. Identify Customer Challenges

When you conduct your marketing study, prepare a list of open ended questions for discussion. Being prepared with your list helps save the valuable time of the participants.

You don't want to rush through the questions but you do want to be considerate of their time. A bulleted list of well thought out questions will get all the information you need to strategize your next marketing campaign.

## Step 5. Do A Competitive Analysis

The last step in the research is to do some competitive analysis to find out exactly what your competition is doing.

Find out things like, how much of the market do they have? How do their products compare to yours? Are there any parts of the market that they are not servicing well?

This information is important to help you establish the one unique selling proposition that you can claim. It is good to know where you stand against your competitors.

Once you've conducted all your marketing research, compile it into a nicely structured report to be used as reference for all your marketing efforts.

Hopefully, by doing the marketing research, you will have uncovered new opportunities that you didn't see before, and can use this information to service your clients better by producing better products.

# Chapter Eleven: Website Development

Developing your web presence is the most central point of building a professional web presence. Owning your own website is like having your own piece of digital property from which to build your digital business.

No longer is brick and mortar, now it's characters and pixels that house your goods and services. With the proper foundation from which to build, you can establish the type of structure that will attract customers to your door.

## What A Website Provides

What exactly are the benefits of having a website? Questions like that usually come from people who are contemplating developing one. If you already have one, you probably already know firsthand what some of them are. But just in case, below are a list of some of the top benefits?

1.  **Business Credibility:** Having a website establishes you as a serious player in the new

digital marketplace. If you've taken the time and expense of creating a site, you have set yourself up as a credible business entity.

2. **Wider Demographic Reach:** A website avails you to more than just your local demographic, but makes your presence available around the world. With this site you can better target who you are trying to reach.

3. **Customer Convenience:** From the customers' point of view, finding information is paramount. Having your website filled with valuable information arranged for easy reference is what they are looking for. You can provide that convenience for them.

4. **Cost Effectiveness:** Cost effectiveness goes both ways. The costs of creating your website is a small investment in relation to the number of increased sales you can make. And from the customers perspective the costs to buy from you are reduced, if they can get what they need from your website.

5. **24/7 Marketing:** This website can act as your 24/7 marketing machine that keeps your name in front of millions of people everyday. Imagine how powerful that can be.

6. **Customer Relationship Building**: When set up correctly, your website can help build stronger relationships with your customers. You can make it easy for them to communicate with you in many different ways, and even solicit feedback from them.

These are just a few of the benefits your website has. The possibilities are dependent on how well you want to meet your customer's needs. Your website is your piece of property in the digital sphere, so build it around aiding your customers in making smart buying decisions.

## How To Build Your New Website

Website building has changed drastically for the better. Now there is technology that makes it easier and faster to get set up. It can sound intimidating at first, but you will find that every piece is very manageable for anyone.

## Step 1. Web Hosting

If you think of web hosting in terms of creating a document on your computer, you can easily grasp its meaning. To create a document on your computer, you open up a word processing program, type in your text, and save it on your hard drive.

To access the information in that document, you have to open the word processing program, find the document on your hard drive, and open the document. The computer hard drive is where you store your files on your computer.

The web hosting company acts like a computer hard drive to store your website files. When you want to open a web site file, you have to go to the computer that stores your file to open it, which in this case is your web hosting company.

The difference is that the computer that the hosting company uses can be accessed by anyone on the Internet.

The amount of files you can store on the hosting company's hard drive is dependent on what hosting packages are available. Each package has different amounts of storage that you can buy.

Hosting companies offer additional services that fit different website needs. But the most important feature of a hosting company is their reliability. You want to ensure that their computers will be available 24/7.
Or at least have minimum downtime.

The next step is purchasing a domain name.

## Step 2. Domain Name

The domain name is what people will type in their web browser to find you. That name should be short and describes what it is you do. These names must be checked for availability from a domain name registrar.

Memorable names are the best, and easiest for customers to find you. And if you can use words that people would type into a search engine to get their problems solved, this name could help people find you faster.

## Step 3. Install a CMS

CMS stands for Content Management System which is simply a program that allows you to manage the content on your website. All your website files are stored in the web hosting company's storage area. To get to this area to manage your files, the CMS makes it easy. The CMS has an administrative area that will allow you to create web pages and blog posts. You can also add images and videos to your site from this administrative area.

A CMS contains an area that gives you access to additional programs that add even more functionality to your website. This functionality can be things like adding e-commerce to your site so that you can sell products.

Or you may want to provide functionality to allow users to download digital information like ebooks and audio files. There are literally thousands of programs available. There are called plugins.

Along with the administrative portion of the CMS, you can preview your website after each change to see how your customers would navigate it. That way you can fix anything before it gets published to the world.

The CMS is a must for any site owner who wants the advantage of ease of maintenance with endless functionality.

## Step 4. Templates for Branding

Why start building your website from scratch when you can use a predesigned website template that is aesthetically pleasing with functionality ready to use?

CMSs will let you install a website template to speed your development even more. There are free and paid templates that are designed to work with whatever CMS you're using.

These templates are customizable to fit your branding needs. You can add your company logo, change colors, add your own images and video to make it look exactly like you want.

Some templates come with built in functionality like call-to-action banners, customizable menus, photo galleries, and maps for directions to your facility. Templates are a great way to get your site up and running quickly.

## Step 5. Edit Template And Write Content

Even though you start with a template, writing all the content will still be your responsibility. This information can come from your marketing team, or from a content creator.

You may have the skills to write content for the web already. If so, then you already know what goes on each page of your website. But even if you are not a content creator, you can outsource the writing to a freelancer. This may cost some money, but you will get a professional job in return.

Writing for the web is different than writing prose for a book or an article. There are common practices that web content writers use. Some are using short sentences, bulleted lists, and lots of white space.

Making the content easily readable, while providing valuable information is the key.

## Step 6. Marketing Strategy

Once you get the site set up how you'd like, it's time to get some attention on it. Putting together your marketing strategy for getting the word out is the next step.

You may want to use search engine marketing to accomplish this which takes some expertise in SEO and time. This is inexpensive to get going, but it will take time.

A faster method is to do some paid advertising. Google Adwords advertising can generate some targeted traffic to your site a lot faster. Also, a part of your strategy may be to use Facebook ads to spread the word.

These options depend on your audience, your product, and how much of a marketing budget you have. Whichever avenue you take, do not neglect the marketing of your new site.

You will also want to set up some web analytics to measure the effectiveness of your marketing efforts. In this regard, testing your approach to see what is the most profitable is how you can optimize your marketing efforts.

The development of your website design is one of the most important things you can do to position yourself as a leader in your market. And your website should reflect that leadership position.

We have just scratched to surface on the subject of website development. For a more exhaustive coverage of this topic, get my book, *"Website Money Machine"*, where I will show you how to set your site up to make money for you 365 day a year.

# Chapter Twelve:  Social Media Marketing

The power of social media marketing has become a critical part of any ongoing marketing plan for companies who want to develop lasting relationships with your customers

The goal of developing a social media strategy is to outline a plan to not only increase your brand awareness, but to initiate and grow a social following. This takes a plan that includes setting some marketing goals, choosing the right networks to use, and measuring your effectiveness.

Following this strategy will give you the information you need to make sure your effort in the social media platforms is positive for your company. We will look at the steps to get started.

## Step 1. Set Your Goals for Social Media

Setting goals for your social media marketing is the first step in building your social strategy. These goals are particular to your type of business and will be the driving force behind all your social media decisions.

Goals could be more than one that will be most effective when tied to an overall business objective. They could be anything from increasing company awareness, generating new leads, increasing website traffic, or to improve your customer support. One common goal among most companies is to increase sales.

Of course you will want to make sure your goals are concrete and measurable so that you can track the result. Many companies use the SMART method (Specific, Measurable, Achievable, Relevant, and Time-bound) for their goal setting approach.

## Step 2. Choose The Right Social Media Channels For You

Choosing the right channel to invest in has a lot to do with where your customers spend their time. Knowing your target audience is the key to help you decide. You want to be where your customers are hanging out.

A quick caution though, you do not have to be on every channel to be effective. A good strategy is to start with the one that the majority of your clients use, and master that. See if you can accomplish your goals with that one channel.

Not all channels are suited for your company, and you will want to decide which works best for you.

If you need more help deciding, then do some competitive research to find out what your competitors are targeting. You can do a quick Google search, and see which channels they advertise on their site.

Once you choose which channels you want, then set up an account to get started. There is a sign-up button on the home page where you can get started filling in all of your account information. That's the easiest way to get started.

## Step 3. Building Your Social Presence

Setting up your account will depend on which platform you decide, but after you do, you will want to start filling out your business information. As example, if you were setting up a Facebook Account you would go through these initial tasks:

- Enter your business information which provides an overview of your business, your contact details, and a link to your website.

- Upload the image for your profile image which can be something recognizable, like your logo or a head shot. Make sure your images are the proper sizes and display well on desktop and mobile views. Look up Facebook's preferred size for the images.

- Create your first post. Make sure you present a good first impression for the people who arrive on your page. Your first post can be something simple like: Welcome to [your business name] Facebook Page! Like our Page if you are a fan of …. [whatever content you will provide].

- To get the ball rolling, follow your contacts which could be your customers who have just purchased products from you and you know will Like and Follow your page.

## Step 4. Create A Social Media Content Calendar

Creating content for your social channel requires not only engaging content, but also content created on a consistent schedule. To make sure you are hitting the mark, companies set up content calendars.

The content calendar schedules all the ideas. This does

not take long to create but will save you the time it takes to come up with these ideas the day you want to publish. When everything is planned out ahead of time, content gets produced on time.

If you are posting content for 15 to 30 minutes of engagement, it is best to have a game plan for what gets posted and who it is targeted. You can create a list of content geared for meeting certain marketing goals. For example, some posts would be to foster engagement, or for educational purposes, and of course, some strictly for making sales.

Content calendars organize your social media content to be distributed on an easy to follow schedule. Make sure to take the time to put one together for your business.

## Step 5. Promoting Your Social Media Channels

Promoting your social media channel is the next step. To do this, all you have to do is get the word out about your page or channel, and encourage people to follow you. Having great posts that encourage sharing can boost your engagement rate. There are other ways to promote your channel.

Here are some other places you can promote your channels:

- Adding buttons to your social channels so website visitors can easily find your social accounts is a great way to make it easy for people to find you.

- Your email list is another place to get the word out. If you don't have your email list started, now is your opportunity. Then, include buttons to your social channels in the footer of every email you send.

- Speaking of email, your email signature is another

marketing opportunity. All you have to do is add social media links to your email signature. Costs you nothing.

- Encourage your staff to follow your social media channels and invite their audience to do the same. If you don't have staff, you can invite your audiences to follow you.

- You can run paid ads to get in front of new audience members. Running ads make sense when there is a clear path to make sales from your networks.

## Step 6. Measure and Optimize

To see how well you are doing with your social media goals, now is the time to measure the results. Once we see the results, we can begin to optimize them for even better performance.

The results to measure are tied to the goals we've set

but there are a few important ones we can consider.

The number of followers we've added is a good measure to look at. Has that number increased based on a certain type of content, and if so can you add even more to raise those numbers?

What about looking at the number of likes, comments, and shares. Are people actually engaging with the content you're posting. Those numbers will vary from week-to-week and post-to-post. But you can begin to watch for trends that you can take advantage of.

Of the links that you post, how many people are actually clicking on those links. This is called your click-thru rate. Measure this in relation to the number of people who see the link as opposed to the ones that see and click the link. This click-thru means that people are engaged enough to take action.

Optimizing your content is based on the data that you collect for your metrics. If content is bringing great results, then you can modify your content schedule to add more of that type of content.

Also, direct customer feedback can reveal information about how you can optimize better based on listening to what the customer wants. They will have their own opinion on what appeals to them.

Companies that meet with their customers can quickly gather this type of data just by adding a few key questions to their conversations. Ask about what content is most useful, and how often would they like to receive it. Find out what channels they want to engage with you on. Make adjustments to your strategy based on their feedback.

## Step 7. Running Paid Ads

If you can justify a business reason for running paid ads on the social platforms, like promoting a product or a program, then ads make a viable consideration for you. These social advertising features help you sell more products and increase your customer reach at the same time.

Refer to your metrics to see what the customers are responding to most, and then build your advertising campaigns around that type of content. You may be able to reuse some content that you've already created, saving your time and money.

The advantage of using these advertising platforms is that you can use the power of the data they collect to do some very specific targeting. It's possible to create different targeting profiles that you want to reach. There are tools to create the ads and help you place them in front of the right audiences.

Ideas for creating promotions to increase sales and company reach center around these promotion types:

- Discounts and coupons – Give your audience a great incentive to want to do business with you right away. Everyone loves to save a little money off the things they want to buy.

- New product launches – Drive your customers through the sales cycle by launching new product promotions that raise awareness and may generate pre-sales.

- Incentives for new customers – Offering incentives for your customers is a great way to introduce new customers to your product, and services. Once they make their first purchase, you can engage them through your social media channel.

- Downloadable e-books and case studies – E-books and case studies are a good tool to demonstrate to your customers your position of authority in your niche. These resources can give valuable information to a targeted audience, and help aid the buying decision.

- Webinar/event promotions – Promotion to encourage the attendance of webinars and special promotional events geared to increase attendance for your upcoming event which give you the opportunity to make sales and offer them to join your community.

- Giveaways – Giveaways with great prizes attract large numbers of prospects who could interact with your company, at least for as long as the giveaway lasts. Care must be taken to ensure that customers only want giveaway but are not really interested in further engagement..

Like the old saying goes, with social media, you have to spend money to make money. The paid ads give you a wider reach that actually can convert into sales. Take the time to learn about the advertising platforms of each of the social media channels. Then build a plan for using them.

## Take It One Step At A Time

Building a social media strategy might seem overwhelming, and there is a lot that goes into doing it right. But the best approach is to take it a step at a time. It's impossible to do everything at once.

Take the time to create your plan, and start small to get

started. As time goes on you will become more familiar with each step in the process. Remember you are undertaking a big project with many moving parts. Stay focused and keep track of your progress.

Nothing is perfect right out of the gate, so plan on making corrections along the way. There is alway room for process improvement based on data and observations that validate the numbers.

Be patient with your campaigns, and apply consistency to your efforts. Progress is made one campaign at a time. The important part of social media is to join the conversation.

# Conclusion

I commend you for making it this far. This shows that you're fully invested into making your marketing efforts the best they can be. Getting started requires a considerable amount of education. There are a lot of pieces and parts to this puzzle, and each takes time to learn.

So far we have discussed the benefits of developing your online marketing strategy. Using the overarching business goals, your marketing strategy is developed to support those goals using the marketing channels that make sense for your organizational skills and resources.

Since all our marketing efforts are more centered around our customer, it requires an analysis to discover just what that target market looks like. The more we know about their pains and struggles, the better solutions we can give them.

The importance of creating the ideal customer personas was stressed to ensure that all content and communications that we create is geared specifically towards reaching them.

Our content is definitely King. So knowing how to make the most effective content possible was discussed here. Creating content that resonates with your customers depends on how well you know and understand them. Take the time to study your customers well.

Email marketing is still one of the most viable marketing tools we have at our disposal. With the help of an autoresponder, you can create a very personalized way to market to your customer.

From there, building a community is another way to spread the word about your brand. With a community, direct feedback can keep you on top of what the community needs to keep them as loyal customers.

Reaching your prospects and clients will take some advertising, whether it is organic or paid. Either way, targeting your prospects is the way to get the right customers to your offers.

If you've decided to try your hand at affiliate marketing, we've talked about choosing the right affiliate partners who provide additional products your product mix. This expands your ability to help your customers even more.

Since most people looking to make a purchase online start by typing a word or phase into a search engine, it will serve your company well to invest in search engine marketing (SEO). It can be a totally free way to increase traffic to your site, and the only investment you'll need to make is time and education.

Your reputation on the Internet is one that can be enhanced with some careful thought into how you brand yourself. Determine the message you want to send through your visuals as well as any written communication. You want to distinguish yourself from the competition. Making your brand a recognizable one that speaks directly to your customers is what you want.

This branding is instantly reflected in the quality of your website. Setting your website up so that it reflects your brand is critical. People make judgements about your company's professionalism by visiting your website. Make sure that visit is a memorable one.

Lastly, we talked about the power of using social media to meet your customers where they hang out. You might not be able to be everywhere, but if you pick the right platform that best suits your customer base, this can be a very powerful marketing channel.

## One Final Word Before We Depart

No matter where you are starting, any business must have some fundamentals in place no matter what products you offer or services you deliver.

The following points will help you generate profits for your business now and long into the future. These steps are not hard to perform, but are critical to your online growth. Make sure you set yourself up for success by giving considerable attention to each step.

These are the five key points:

- Business Plan with Goals - Create a flexible business plan that clearly charts the road ahead. Plans do change as time goes on, so visit this plan often and make necessary adjustments.

  Goals are the markers along the way that keep you on track and making progress. Make goals to keep you moving in the direction you want to go. Every accomplished goal inspires you to take on the next.

- Know Your Customers - One of the most beneficial exercises you can do is research your target market. Your knowledge will allow you to create the products that your customers need and want.

  Your understanding of their needs will help you build long-term relations with them and create a loyal following of raving fans.

- Advertise - Advertise to expand your brand and sell more products. The best form for your company depends on many factors. You may take advantage of SEO, or advertise on the social platforms that your customers use. The way to optimize your efforts is to measure your results. The numbers will tell you what you need to do for greater improvements and better results.

- Deliver Results - Delivering on what you promise is a rule that you should never break. Alway deliver on a promise. This is so important to you, I want to repeat it 100 times.

Nothing will ruin your reputation faster than breaking your promise. On the other hand, when you consistently deliver, people tell other people. Your good reputation will quickly spread. Soon you will have so much business that it will be hard to keep up with.

- Maintain Your CRM Database - Developing and maintaining your customer database will serve you for years to come. It will help you see trends in customer behavior that will help you stay on top of changing consumer demand.

It will help you collect and nurture leads that can turn into buying customers. The more leads you convert that more profits you'll make.

Building these principles into your everyday business life will allow you to continually enjoy many years of growth and success.

**It's Time To Start Your Marketing Engines**

Not it's time to start your marketing engine and start driving to your marketing destinations. There is a lot of information in this book, and it will take time to master each part of the marketing process. I recommend that you use this book as a reference. This is your introduction into setting up your marketing with all the basics covered.

It is my recommendation that you always continue your education in marketing and business itself. That education will be the key to making even more profits in the future.

To get a deeper look into things like creating a

dynamic website that helps you make money, consider getting my book *"Website Money Machine"*. It will teach you how to set up your website to work for you 24/7, no matter what your level of technical expertise.

If you are not getting the sales you want, it may be that your sales process is flawed. To get some assistance in the area of sales, get my book *"Success-N-Sales"*. It is your guide to creating explosive sales by helping you build a solid sales foundation. Sales is something that everyone in your company should know. Make sure you get a copy today.

I wish you all the best in all your marketing endeavors.

**Don't forget to visit
WebsiteMarketingMachine.com for the latest
resources to help you along the way.**

# Get More Great Resources

# Website Money Machine

*Making Money with Your Website Has Never Been Easier!*

## Principles for Making Money Online are Revealed

Learning the secrets to make your Website more profitable, boost your traffic, generate more leads, and make more sales online, than you ever dreamed.

Don't be like the companies I know that spend thousands of dollars on advertising, banner ads, website design, and other costs, but still aren't generating any results.

You must have this book!

The information contained in this book really works. It starts you off on the right track by explaining all the concepts and skills required to become a learner in the online arena.

It's not required to be an expert in creating and modifying your website in the beginning, but by the end of the book, you will know what has to be done to keep your site selling for you year after year.

Go to http://www.websitemarketingmachine.com to purchase your copy.

## <u>Success 'N Sales</u>
## The #1 Guide To Explosive
## Success In Sales

## Easy-to-Follow Guide for a Money-Making Career In Sales

*Success'N Sales* is your entrance into the exciting world of selling.

No matter whether you're a beginner or a seasoned veteran, this information in this book will help you sell better. Better sales mean you make better money.

*Success 'N Sales* contains a solid, easy-to-follow, foundation for launching a highly money-making sales career, or simply improving what you already do.

From pre-call planning to closing the sale, and everything in between is covered in detail.

Each chapter ends with a short quiz to test your memory of the chapter contents. When you complete this book, you will be ready to apply your newly discovered skills to boost sales for your company.

It takes the fear out of the entire selling process. You will want to keep this book for your ready reference.

Go to http://www.SuccessNSales.com to learn more.

# Are You A Super Achiever?

# Everything You Need To Know To Become A Great Super Achiever

## Guide to Getting Started on the Road To Super Achievement.

Here you will find everything you need to start achieving more than you've ever dreamed possible, in anything you want to accomplish.

No matter what your circumstances, with this guide you can get on the fastlane to becoming a Super Achiever.

Anyone can be considered a Super Achiever when they take their first step on the road that leads to the accomplishment of their dreams. If they choose to stay on that road to the end, they will succeed.

So many people go through life without a clear vision for what their future will look like. Therefore, they are subject to accepting whatever life brings their way.

"Are You A Super Achiever?" walks you through the method of defining your vision with extreme clarity.

After you are clear, then you set goals to accomplish that dream life you've defined in your vision statement.

From there, your roadmap will get you to your destination with the help of massive action on your part. It works when you work.

**Learn how to get started today!**

**Visit: SuperAchieversNetwork.org**

# About the Author

 Albert L. Powell, Jr. is an entrepreneur who specializes in coaching and consulting for success in business and personal achievement.

Albert's primary objective is to encourage anyone interested in making money with a website to be successful.

Teaching technical or non-technical people to utilize the Internet to realize their dreams, Albert believes anyone can be successful.

Albert has been working in the Information Technology field for 20 years, and now is sharing helpful techniques gained through years of experience in the public and private sectors.

Albert has been developing informational products that are easy to learn by anyone with a desire to succeed.

He maintains a blog on the Super Achievers Network that is filled with articles that motivate and inspire go-getters who are making their mark on the world.

When you get stressed and need a pick-me-up, check out the S.A.N. (Super Achievers Network) blog.

When he's not working, you can find him playing drums with a local band, taking pictures of interesting things he encounters in his travels, or binging on a Netflix series.

Feel free to contact Albert at 304-404-3171 for one-on-one consultation to discuss how you can accomplish your goals.

Visit his personal site at
http://www.AlbertPowellJr.com.

***Your success is his business!***

www.ingramcontent.com/pod-product-compliance
Lightning Source LLC
Chambersburg PA
CBHW030638220526
45463CB00004B/1570